GREAT DISCOVERIES & INVENTIONS

That Improved Human Health

For a free color catalog describing Gareth Stevens Publishing's list of high-quality books and multimedia programs, call 1-800-542-2595 (USA) or 1-800-461-9120 (Canada). Gareth Stevens Publishing's Fax: (414) 332-3567.

The editor would like to extend thanks to Randall Farchmin, science instructor, Milwaukee Area Technical College, Milwaukee, Wisconsin, for his kind and professional help with the information in this book.

Library of Congress Cataloging-in-Publication Data

Casanellas, Antonio.
   [Ser vivo. English]
   Great discoveries and inventions that improved human health / by Antonio Casanellas; illustrated by Ali Garousi.
      p. cm. — (Great discoveries and inventions)
   Includes bibliographical references and index.
   Summary: Traces the history of medicine from early surgery and the discovery of radioactivity to progress in modern medicines and genetic engineering. Includes some simple activities.
   ISBN 0-8368-2585-3 (lib. bdg.)
   1. Medicine—History—Juvenile literature. 2. Medical innovations—Juvenile literature. [1. Medicine—History. 2. Medical innovations.] I. Garousi, Ali, ill. II. Title. III. Series.
R133.5.C3713   2000
610'.9—dc21   99-053261

First published in North America in 2000 by
Gareth Stevens Publishing
A World Almanac Education Group Company
330 West Olive Street, Suite 100
Milwaukee, WI 53212 USA

This U.S. edition © 2000 by Gareth Stevens, Inc. Original edition © 1999 by Ediciones Lema, S.L., Barcelona, Spain. Translated from the Spanish by Flor de Lis Igualada. Photographic composition and photo mechanics: Novasis, S.A.L. Barcelona (Spain). Additional end matter © 2000 by Gareth Stevens, Inc.

Printed in the United States of America

1 2 3 4 5 6 7 8 9 04 03 02 01 00

Gareth Stevens Publishing
A WORLD ALMANAC EDUCATION GROUP COMPANY

Modern Diagnostic Methods

The development of medicine for human health has been slow and steady. The diagnostic method was perfected in the nineteenth century. Joseph Skoda, a Czech physician, formulated the guidelines for the process. Today, there are numerous methods for diagnosing an illness. A diagnosis is basically made up of three stages — the observation of the problem, the careful study of anything abnormal in the important organs, and the explanation of the problem based upon the evidence. The illness is then identified, and the corresponding treatment is prescribed. Some modern methods for diagnosing illnesses involve electrocardiograms, blood tests, urine analyses, X-rays, and encephalograms.

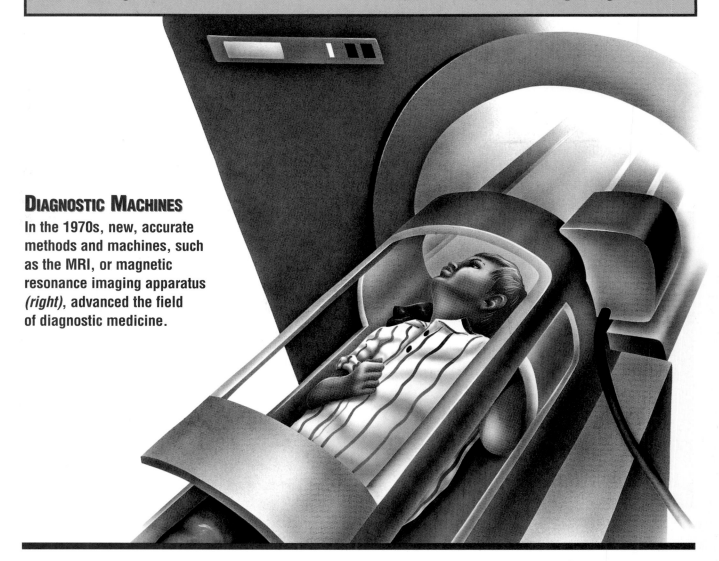

DIAGNOSTIC MACHINES

In the 1970s, new, accurate methods and machines, such as the MRI, or magnetic resonance imaging apparatus *(right)*, advanced the field of diagnostic medicine.

THE DIAGNOSIS OF ILLNESS

By the Middle Ages, people saw that to understand how to cure a specific illness, they first needed to understand how a healthy body operates. To find out about this, the first dissections of human bodies took place. Previously, dissections were strictly forbidden by the Church. Some of the diagnostic methods used today — measuring blood pressure, taking the pulse, and listening to the body with a stethoscope *(left)* — were developed a very long time ago.

IMAGING TEMPERATURE

Thermographic diagnostic methods reveal various body temperatures, highlighting possible tumors.

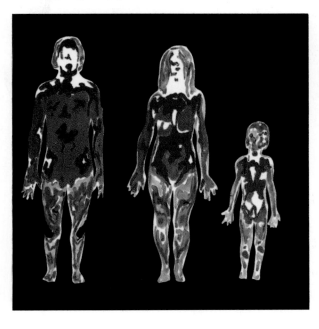

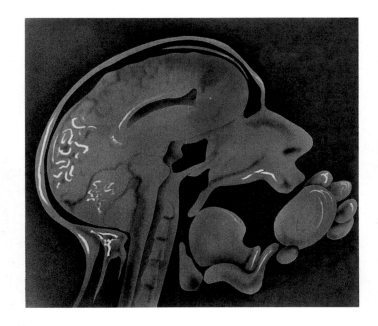

MAGNETIC RESONANCE IMAGING

Through magnetic resonance, it is possible to obtain very clear images of the inside of a human body. The images are produced using powerful magnets.

Radioisotopes

At the end of the nineteenth century, Marie and Pierre Curie, married scientists working in France, made revolutionary discoveries in the field of radioactivity. She was a Polish physicist and mathematician, and he was a French physicist. From Marie Curie's early research, further important medical findings developed, particularly in the field of radioisotopes. Radioisotopes can make tumors smaller or cure them without surgery. The tumors are destroyed through gamma-ray radiation. The field of archaeology also uses radioisotopes. Scientists determine the age of rocks by analyzing the isotopes they contain. Calculations using radioisotopes seem to show that the Earth is about 4.5 billion years old! The Curies' work also led to understanding the structure of the atom, which releases enormous amounts of energy when split.

RADIOACTIVITY

Radioactivity is the emission of energy particles. This radiation can cause air to conduct electricity. Marie Curie studied radioactive elements, using a piezo-electroscope *(right)* invented by her husband and his brother to detect weak electrical currents. She coined the term *radioactivity* and found that it comes from the atoms of certain elements. Marie Curie discovered two new elements: radium and polonium. She won two Nobel prizes: for physics in 1903 and for chemistry in 1911. Her work led to radioactive treatment for some diseases, such as cancer.

Pierre Curie's 1880 piezo-electroscope, which measured surface electric charges of compressed quartz crystals

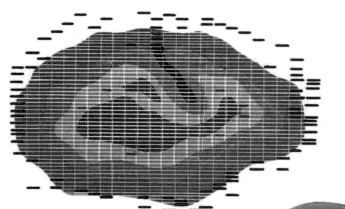

TRACING SUBSTANCES

If radioisotopes of certain elements are injected into the body, it is possible to follow the path of the elements inside the body. In the illustration *(left)*, a large amount of sulfur in the liver is visible. The red areas indicate the highest concentrations, and the blue areas indicate lower concentrations.

LINEAR ACCELERATOR

Linear accelerators, such as this one *(right)*, are large machines that emit gamma rays in the form of very thin beams. Gamma rays reduce or destroy internal tumors without the need for surgery.

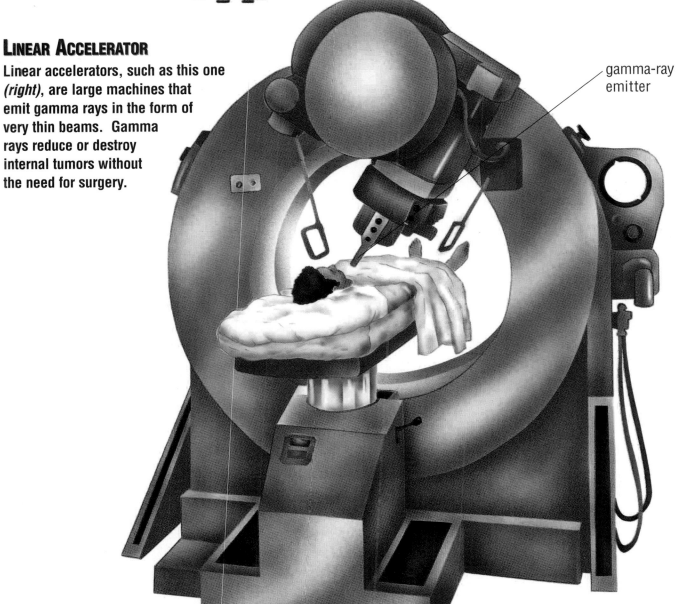

gamma-ray emitter

Transplants and Implants

Some of medicine's most spectacular developments have taken place in the field of surgery, particularly in the area of transplants. Transplants involve removing an organ from one person and surgically placing it into the body of another. Today, it is possible to transplant various organs, such as the kidney. Perhaps the best-known organ to be transplanted is the heart.

The first human heart transplant took place in 1967 in Cape Town, South Africa. Dr. Christiaan Barnard succeeded in replacing a large portion of an unhealthy heart with the corresponding part of a healthy heart. Implant surgery is different from transplant surgery. Implants are artificially made and then surgically placed into the body.

SURGERY

At the beginning of the sixteenth century, surgery was performed without anesthesia, often by barbers, who also pulled teeth. Surgical techniques have continually improved. Ambroise Paré was one of the most famous surgeons of the sixteenth century. While in the army, he created an ointment for treating injuries. At this time, wounds were usually sealed off, or cauterized, with hot irons, a painful and damaging procedure. Paré also designed wooden arms, hands, and legs.

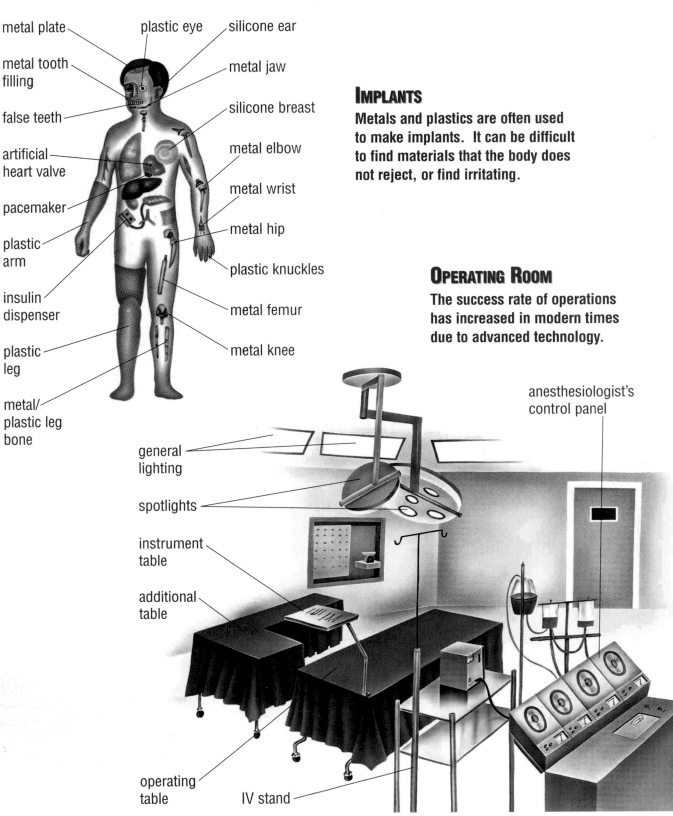

metal plate

plastic eye

silicone ear

metal tooth filling

metal jaw

false teeth

silicone breast

artificial heart valve

metal elbow

pacemaker

metal wrist

plastic arm

metal hip

insulin dispenser

plastic knuckles

plastic leg

metal femur

metal/ plastic leg bone

metal knee

IMPLANTS

Metals and plastics are often used to make implants. It can be difficult to find materials that the body does not reject, or find irritating.

OPERATING ROOM

The success rate of operations has increased in modern times due to advanced technology.

anesthesiologist's control panel

general lighting

spotlights

instrument table

additional table

operating table

IV stand

Modern Cardiology

William Harvey, an English doctor who lived in the seventeenth century, first described the heart as a pump that circulates blood through the body. Blood always moves in the same direction. It leaves the heart through the arteries, travels to all the organs of the body, and returns to the heart through veins. However, heart cells that stimulate heartbeats sometimes become damaged. To solve this problem, battery-powered pacemakers that artificially generate heartbeats are implanted into the body. The artificial pacemaker was invented by Wilson Greatbatch in 1958. Currently, circulatory diseases are among the most serious and common health problems in the Western world.

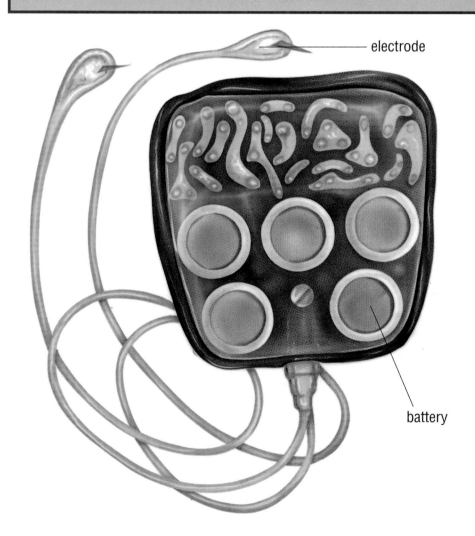

electrode

battery

EARLY PACEMAKER

Current pacemakers are about the size of a quarter. In the past, they were large, inconvenient devices with batteries that needed to be changed frequently. Today, a pacemaker's batteries keep working for more than ten years at a time.

match
(for size comparison)

FIRST TRANSFUSION ATTEMPTS

By the end of the seventeenth century, blood transfusions tried between animals and humans usually resulted in the death of the patient.

ELECTROCARDIOGRAPH

The electrocardiograph explores electrical activity in the heart. Electrodes are attached to a patient's wrist, elbow, knee, and chest. The electrocardiograph registers any electrical impulses it detects and records them on paper.

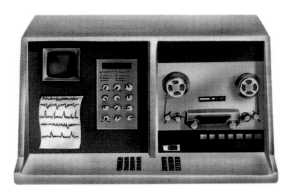

BLOOD CIRCULATION

During the Renaissance, many of the classic theories of medicine were discovered. One of the most important events was William Harvey's discovery of the system of blood circulation — the heart pumps blood, and the blood always travels in the same direction. In the illustration below, the red and blue colors indicate oxygen levels in the blood.

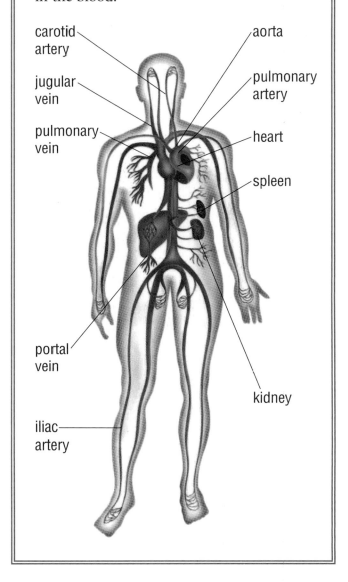

carotid artery
aorta
jugular vein
pulmonary artery
pulmonary vein
heart
spleen
portal vein
kidney
iliac artery

Vaccines and Antibiotics

In the mid-1800s, French chemist Louis Pasteur discovered that certain microbes, or germs, carry and cause disease. This finding was the basis for the invention of vaccination. Pasteur and other scientists created vaccines to fight many terrible epidemic diseases, such as tetanus, tuberculosis, and cholera. At the beginning of the twentieth century, English bacteriologist Alexander Fleming discovered the first antibiotic — penicillin. Penicillin saved many soldiers' lives during World War II by reducing infection in injuries. In recent years, many new antibiotics have been developed. They cure diseases that are caused by bacteria. Antibiotics have no effect on diseases caused by viruses, however. Researchers believe that vaccination is the only way to fight against some contagious diseases, such as polio and AIDS.

FIRST PENICILLIN CURE

Early in the twentieth century, Alexander Fleming was experimenting with penicillin when a friend fell ill with meningitis. Fleming injected him with the only penicillin dose he had, and saved his life. It was the first time that penicillin was used with a human being.

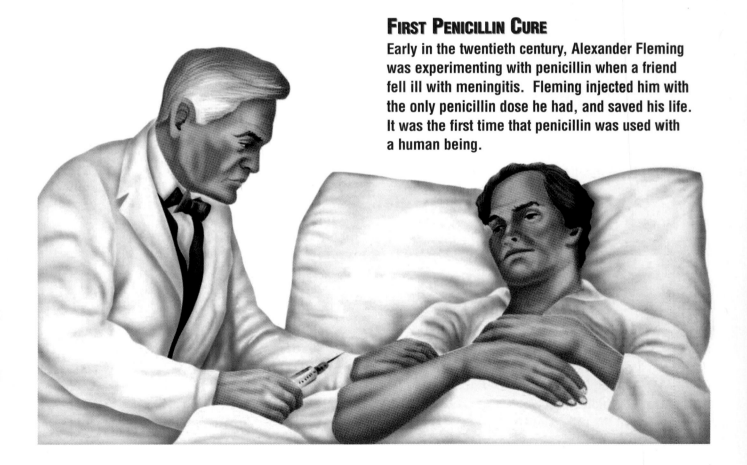

VACCINATIONS

In 1796, Edward Jenner gave the first actual smallpox vaccination. The event was not taken seriously, and another fifty years passed before Louis Pasteur scientifically proved how vaccines work. The steps in the vaccination process include the following: first, germs that cause a particular illness are isolated and weakened or destroyed so they are not harmful. Then, those germs are injected into a person. The person's body produces antibody molecules and specialized defense cells that are programmed to fight the germs. The antibody-producing cells and defense cells remain in the person's body to defend against future infections from that particular type of germ.

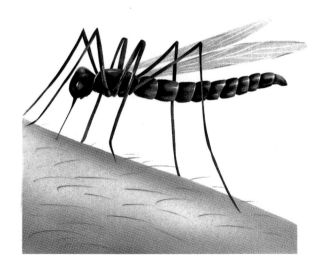

mold surrounding bacteria

bacteria

MALARIA

Malaria is a disease caused by a one-celled parasite. It is spread through the bite of a mosquito *(below)*. A vaccine for malaria is currently being developed.

ANTIBIOTIC DISCOVERY

Alexander Fleming found mold contaminating some bacteria culture plates *(above)*. He observed that a substance from the mold stopped the bacteria from growing. Fleming then isolated penicillin in 1928.

CAT Scanner

Much of the time, doctors can quickly diagnose the particular ailments from which a patient suffers. It is rarely necessary to cut into and open the human body to reach a diagnosis. Doctors use advances in medical technology, such as computer-controlled X-rays, to see inside the body without cutting. The CAT (computer axial tomography) scanner is one of the most modern methods of medical observation. This apparatus transmits rotating or reflected X-ray beams through the human body. A receptor records the resulting signals. A doctor then interprets the signals to reach a diagnosis.

CAT SCANNER
The CAT scanner visually records a cross section of an area of the body.

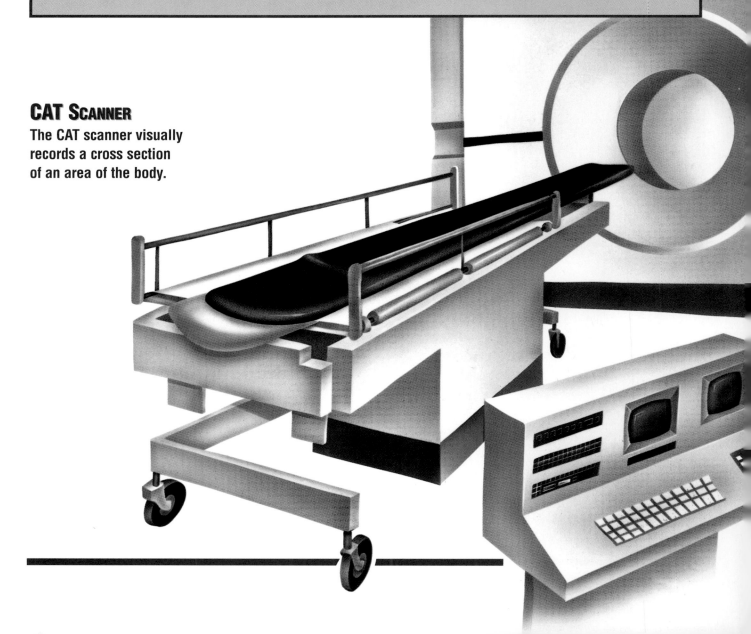

X-Rays

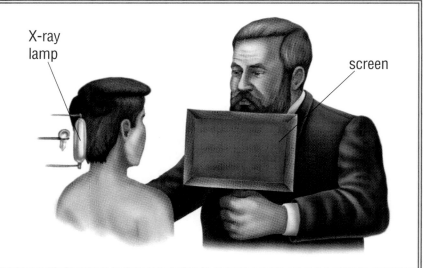

X-ray lamp

screen

X-rays are produced by cathode ray tubes or vacuum tubes. Electrons leave the cathode (negative electrode) and strike the plate-shaped metal anode (positive electrode). High-energy X-rays are produced when the electrons strike the solid material of the anode. The earliest radiographic machine *(right)* was hand-held.

X-rays pass through the body's soft tissues, but they are absorbed by the bones. Doctors can then examine the resulting film of the bones *(right)*.

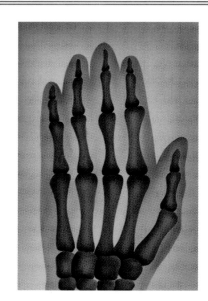

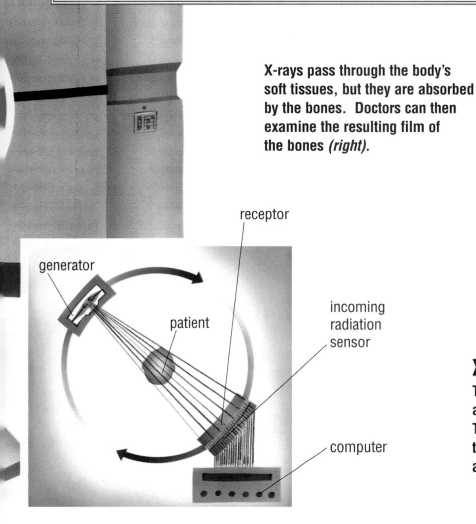

receptor

generator

patient

incoming radiation sensor

computer

X-Ray Transmission

The X-ray generator and receptor *(left)* are located opposite each another. The X-rays produce an electric current that is then processed by a computer and transformed into an image *(above)*.

DNA

At the beginning of the twentieth century, scientists already understood that living beings contain genes that are located in chromosomes in the body. The structure of a gene remained a mystery, however. Scientists eventually discovered that chromosomes contain DNA and proteins. DNA, or deoxyribonucleic acid, appears in every cell of a living body. In the 1950s, scientists discovered that DNA was responsible for transmitting hereditary characteristics from one generation to the next. DNA contains all the body's physical characteristics, such as hair and eye color, as well as some of the person's psychological and personality characteristics.

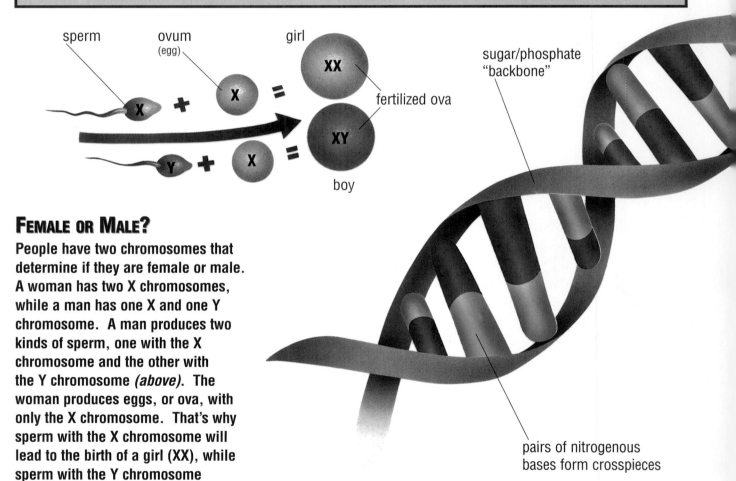

sperm
ovum (egg)
girl
XX
fertilized ova
XY
boy
sugar/phosphate "backbone"
pairs of nitrogenous bases form crosspieces

FEMALE OR MALE?

People have two chromosomes that determine if they are female or male. A woman has two X chromosomes, while a man has one X and one Y chromosome. A man produces two kinds of sperm, one with the X chromosome and the other with the Y chromosome *(above)*. The woman produces eggs, or ova, with only the X chromosome. That's why sperm with the X chromosome will lead to the birth of a girl (XX), while sperm with the Y chromosome will lead to the birth of a boy (XY).

DNA DOUBLE HELIX CHAIN

DNA is in the shape of a double helix, resembling a twisted ladder. Six chemicals make up the two side-strands (or backbones) and the four bases of the DNA. The bases form pairs that cross-connect the side-strands to make the "rungs" of the ladder.

HUMAN CHROMOSOMES

Every cell in the human body contains forty-six chromosomes. They are curled into a spiral that would measure 6.6 feet (2 meters) long if stretched out.

THE CELL

Every cell in the human body, though ten times smaller than a pin-hole, performs a specific function, depending on the tissue in which it is located. Every type of cell is different. Chromosomes, located in the nucleus of a cell, contain DNA, which is divided into small units called genes. These genes transmit the characteristics of each species and each individual. Each gene consists of dozens to thousands of the four nitrogenous bases (adenine, guanine, cytosine, and thymine). These bases are arranged in specific patterns along the DNA and provide information to produce chemical materials the cells need. Human beings have over 100,000 genes. Other mammals have 50,000 to 100,000 genes.

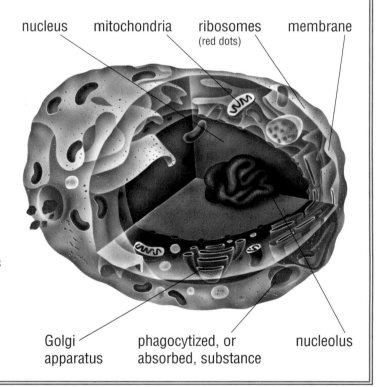

nucleus   mitochondria   ribosomes (red dots)   membrane

Golgi apparatus   phagocytized, or absorbed, substance   nucleolus

Artificial Selection

Each member of any animal or plant species inherits certain characteristics from its ancestors. English naturalist Charles Darwin and Austrian botanist Gregor Mendel developed theories of evolution explaining how all plants and animals have evolved from earlier living species. The theories allowed scientists to later breed animals and plants to fit particular needs. The best plants and animals could be chosen and then crossbred for even better-quality plants and animals. This process is called artificial selection, or selective breeding. For example, when artificial selection is used, cows produce more milk, and plants produce more food, grow faster, and resist diseases or extreme climates more easily.

CROSSBREEDING CORN

Two hybrid plants can be crossed to increase production. The steps are repeated with the next generation of seeds.

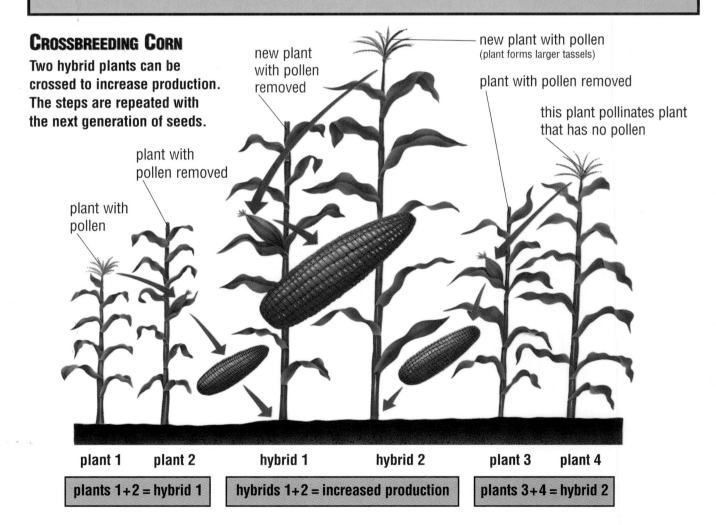

new plant with pollen removed

new plant with pollen
(plant forms larger tassels)

plant with pollen removed

this plant pollinates plant that has no pollen

plant with pollen removed

plant with pollen

| plant 1 | plant 2 | hybrid 1 | hybrid 2 | plant 3 | plant 4 |

| plants 1+2 = hybrid 1 | hybrids 1+2 = increased production | plants 3+4 = hybrid 2 |

seedless
tomato

seedless
orange

SEEDLESS PRODUCE

Plants and animals can be genetically changed to achieve certain goals. These methods can create, for instance, tomatoes and oranges without seeds.

SELECTIVE BREEDING

A great many genetic studies have been made in recent years. Artificial selection has led to cows that produce more milk than ever before.

GENETIC VARIATION AND MUTATION

Evolutionary changes in plants and animals happen in two ways — from differences in the combination of the characteristics of their parents and through mutation. Mutation means a sudden change in the gene. Most mutations are harmful to the plant or animal. Changes that help an organism survive are inherited by the next generation. Animals and plants belonging to the same species inherit some characteristics from their evolutionary predecessors. Human beings are members of the order of mammals called primates.

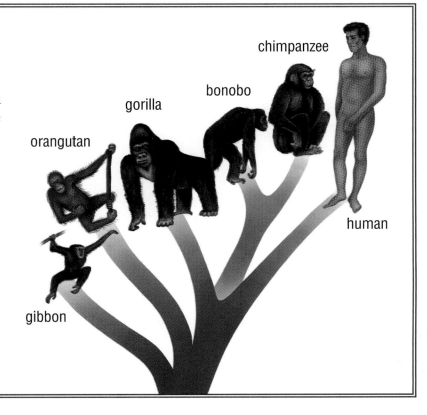

chimpanzee

bonobo

gorilla

orangutan

human

gibbon

Genetic Engineering

Because biologists now know the structure of DNA, which transmits hereditary traits, they can do genetic engineering. With this technology, scientists can transfer a characteristic that belongs to one particular species of plant or animal to a completely different one. The process requires isolating the gene responsible for one specific function and transferring it to another organism, thereby creating a new variety of organism. Genetic engineering is used to develop resistance to many hereditary diseases. It can increase survival in harsh environments. It is used in the breeding of plants and animals to improve the size and quality of the new plants and animals that grow. Genetics is also important in research fields, such as molecular biology, where biological processes are analyzed.

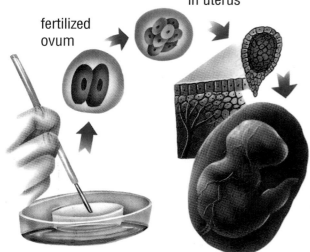

fertilized ovum

embryo placed in uterus

fully developed embryo

TEST TUBE PREGNANCY

When a woman wants to get pregnant but cannot do so naturally, her ovum, or egg, can be removed and brought into contact with sperm outside her body. The fertilized ovum develops into an embryo and can then be placed into the woman's uterus to grow into a baby.

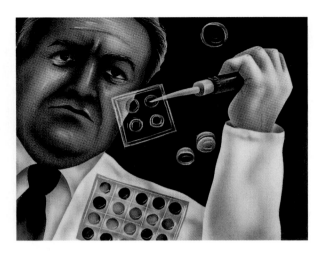

Insulin is a hormone produced in the pancreas. It keeps the level of usable blood sugar in the body balanced. Through the cloning process, the gene that orders insulin to be produced is isolated and implanted into bacteria called *Escherichia coli*. These bacteria then start producing insulin.

CLONING

The frogs *(left)* have been cloned. They were produced using an unfertilized frog ovum and the tissue of a tadpole's intestine.

MENDEL'S LAWS

Modern genetic engineering developed based on Austrian monk Gregor Mendel's nineteenth-century discovery of the laws of heredity. Mendel grew peas in the garden of his monastery. Some were yellow, and others were green. He fertilized the flowers of the green peas with pollen from the yellow ones, and vice versa. After that, he crossed the new peas. His observations are illustrated below: one kind of pea was dominant.

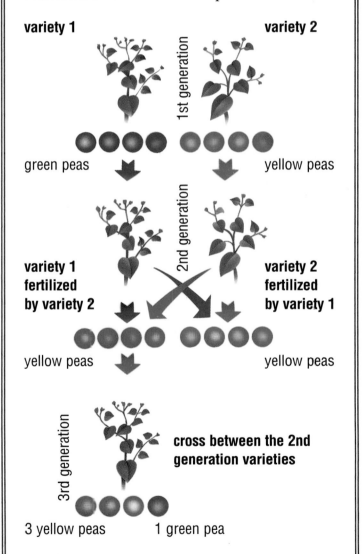

variety 1 · variety 2 · 1st generation · green peas · yellow peas · 2nd generation · variety 1 fertilized by variety 2 · variety 2 fertilized by variety 1 · yellow peas · yellow peas · 3rd generation · cross between the 2nd generation varieties · 3 yellow peas · 1 green pea

Modern Medicines

During the Renaissance, physician and chemist Paracelsus disproved the common belief that illness was caused by the imbalance of body fluids. In the early sixteenth century, he showed that each illness is, in fact, a specific and definable disorder. He suggested the use of chemicals to treat various illnesses. This was how the modern-day science of pharmacology began. Today, thousands of different medicines are produced, providing relief and cures for many illnesses. The majority of the 25,000 medicines in existence are obtained from microorganisms or manufactured in chemical laboratories. In addition, some medicines are obtained from natural plants, animals, and minerals.

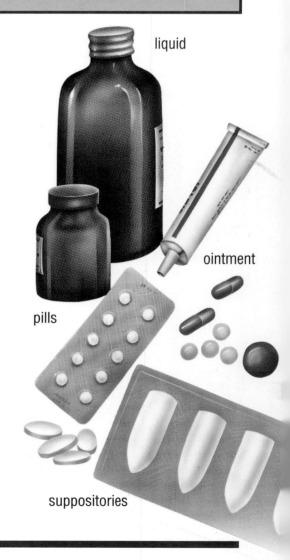

liquid

ointment

pills

suppositories

COWPOX
Cowpox is a mild skin disease that affects cattle. In earlier times, many people who worked with the diseased cows *(above)* caught the disease. Once these people recovered from cowpox, they discovered they were now immune to smallpox and never caught that dangerous disease. This discovery led to the development of vaccination.

EARLY MEDICINES

Early medicines were extracted from minerals, plants, and animals. Doctors recorded each substance in lists called pharmacopoeias. For example, the pychra herbal was listed as a compound made up of spices, aloes, and other herbs. The active ingredients in herbs were later found and manufactured in pure form. Other drugs were made from chemicals. Today's pharmaceutical industry still searches for naturally-occurring medicines whose active ingredients can be manufactured.

nux vomica

hyssop

hellebore

morning glory

EARLY DRUGSTORES

Before modern times, pharmacies *(left)* stocked porcelain bottles containing the ingredients for making medicines.

TYPES OF MEDICINES

Medicines are available in various forms. Most medicines are taken orally (by mouth).

capsules

TESTING DRUGS

Researchers observe the effects of medicines on mice and rabbits kept in laboratories *(right)*. Some people now disagree with this type of research.

The Eye

YOU WILL NEED:

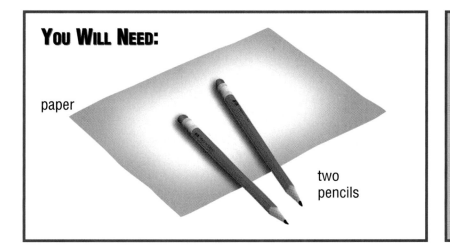

paper

two pencils

Ophthalmology is a branch of medicine that deals with the eyes and eye diseases. Medical research has resulted in successful treatments and new ways to improve vision.

The following projects show how the brain blends images, how pupils react to light, where the eye does not detect images, and how eyes perceive three dimensions.

PROJECT 1: BLENDING IMAGES

1. Roll a piece of paper into a tube *(as shown).*

2. Hold your hand in front of one eye and look through the tube with the other eye. Keep both eyes open. Move your hand close to the tube. Do you see a hole in your hand? Your brain blends the image from each eye into one image.

PROJECT 2:
REACTING TO LIGHT

1. In a dimly lit place, look at the pupil in a friend's eye.

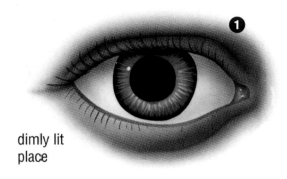

dimly lit place

well-lit place

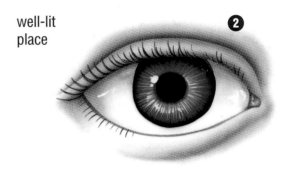

2. In a well-lit place, look at your friend's pupil again. It has become smaller because the eye regulates how much light can enter it.

PROJECT 3:
THE OPTIC DISK

★

The eye is connected to the brain by the optic nerve, which is located behind the eyeball. There are no cells sensitive to light at the point of this connection (the optic disk). Therefore, light that falls there cannot be seen.

●

1. Close your left eye and stare at the star.

2. Slowly move the page close to your right eye, still looking at the star.

3. Stop when the dot disappears. The dot is now in line with the optic disk, which cannot perceive the image.

PROJECT 4:
SEEING IN 3-D

1. Hold a pencil in each hand, so that their points touch. Now separate them.

2. Stretch out both arms and close one eye.

3. Try to connect the two pencil points as you did before. It is more difficult now because one eye alone cannot judge distance, which is needed to see in three dimensions.

When objects are viewed with both eyes, the objects have three dimensions. When only one eye is used, distances cannot be perceived.

Surface Tension

YOU WILL NEED:

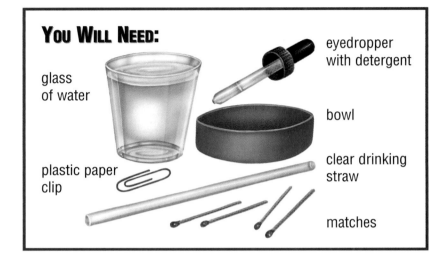

glass of water

plastic paper clip

eyedropper with detergent

bowl

clear drinking straw

matches

Water makes up two-thirds of the human body and has always been a necessary part of medicine. One of the most important characteristics of water is its surface tension. See for yourself how surface tension works with the following project. The body has a method for preventing the health problems that surface tension might cause in the lungs.

PROJECT 1:

1. Fill a glass with water and carefully put a paper clip onto the surface of the water. Using a tweezers makes this easier.

2. You will see that the paper clip floats. The water molecules attract one another, and the surface of the water forms a kind of "skin." Look carefully to see how this skin expands under the clip.

❶

❷

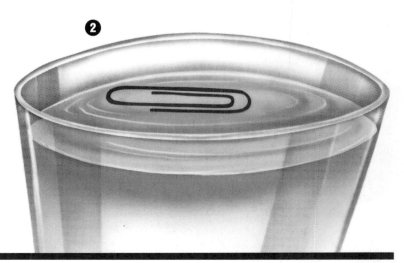

❶

PROJECT 2:

1. Place a drinking straw in the glass of water. The pressure that surface tension puts upon water when it is forced into a narrow tube is called capillarity.

2. Look at the water inside the straw. It is curved and higher than the rest of the water in the glass.

❷

PROJECT 3:

1. Detergents lower the surface tension of water. To understand this, float some matches or wooden toothpicks in a bowl of water.

2. Put a few drops of detergent in the center of the bowl. The detergent decreases the surface tension in the center and increases it at the edges, dragging the matches outward. Cells in the walls of the air sacs (alveoli) of the lungs produce a "detergent" that keeps the walls of the air sacs from sticking together and collapsing.

❶

❷

Capillarity

YOU WILL NEED:

red, blue, and green food coloring

white carnations

three glasses of water

Plant and animal bodies must move fluids. Human bodies move blood through tiny capillaries. Vascular plants, or plants with channels through which water flows, also depend on capillarity to transport fluid. Capillarity is the pressure surface tension puts on a liquid forced into a narrow tube. This pressure pushes the liquid up through the tube. The following projects will show you capillarity at work in plant stems.

PROJECT 1:

1. Pour some of each food coloring into different glasses. The water will become red, blue, and green.

2. Put a white carnation into each glass.

3. After a few days, you will see that the color of each carnation's petals has changed to the same color as the water. That is because capillarity caused the water to rise through the stem to the petals and dye them.

PROJECT 2:

This project illustrates capillarity — using two colors and one flower.

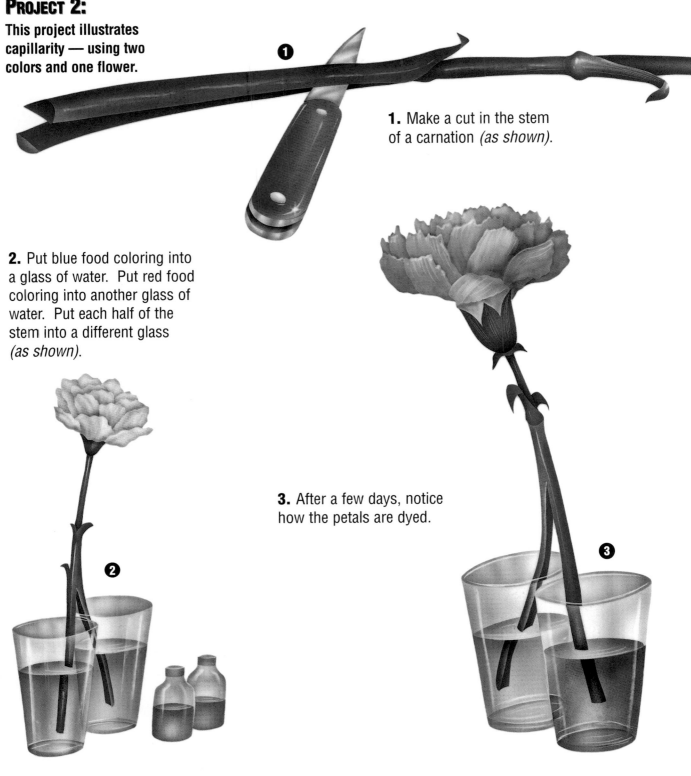

1. Make a cut in the stem of a carnation *(as shown)*.

2. Put blue food coloring into a glass of water. Put red food coloring into another glass of water. Put each half of the stem into a different glass *(as shown)*.

3. After a few days, notice how the petals are dyed.

Cloning

YOU WILL NEED:

plant container

planting mix

potato

glass jar

Potato plants grow from fat roots, or tubers, underground and develop into blooming plants. The plants produce tubers with different DNA. From only one potato, or even just a piece of one, you can obtain many more tubers. The new plants will have the same DNA and genes as the parent and as each other. This is a process similar to cloning. Produce identical tubers with this project.

1. Fill two-thirds of a jar with water.

2. Place a potato on top of the jar, making sure that the end of the potato touches the water. In a few days, buds will appear.

3. Remove all of the buds except the strongest two.

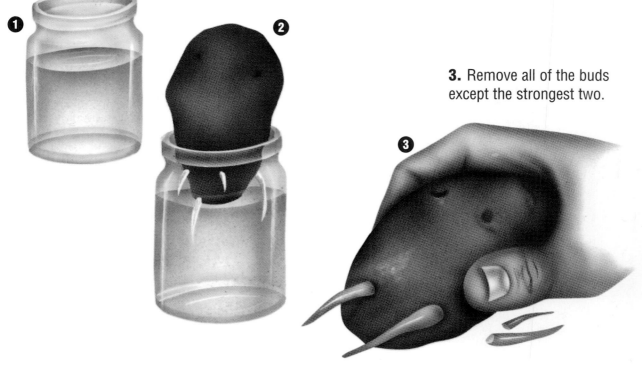

4. Fill the plant container halfway with planting mix. Bury the potato in the container. Keep the soil damp at all times.

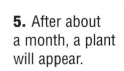

5. After about a month, a plant will appear.

6. Add fresh planting mix to what is already in the container.

7. When flowers appear on the plant, stop watering it or else the potatoes will rot. When the plant dries up, carefully pull it out and see how many potatoes have grown — probably more than four.

Glossary

abnormality: irregularity; a mistake or an unhealthy change in what is expected.

anesthesia: a substance that numbs the nerves to prevent the feeling of pain.

aorta: the largest artery, which carries blood from the heart to other arteries and thus to the body's other parts.

capillarity: the rise or fall of a fluid between two walls due to surface tension and the weight of the fluid.

cathode rays: streams of electrons that a negative electrode produces in a glass vacuum tube.

cloning: producing identical offspring or copies of an organism by using a cell from that organism that is not a seed cell.

computer axial tomography (CAT): a method of diagnosis that uses X-rays to produce three-dimensional images.

dissection: the cutting up of a dead body for medical study of its internal parts and how they fit together.

electrocardiograms: records that reveal possible heart problems shown by changes of electrical signals during the heartbeat.

electroscope: an instrument that measures small amounts of electrical charge.

encephalograms: X-rays of the brain.

evolution: changes in a species over time that allow better survival in its environment.

genes: sections of DNA that carry instructions for specific inherited traits.

Golgi apparatus: a specialized part of a cell that changes chemicals and packages them in internal membranes.

hybrid: an offspring of two animals or plants of different varieties or species. Hybrids are not able to reproduce.

insulin: a hormone the body needs to digest and use sugars or carbohydrates.

isotope: Similar atoms with a difference in the number of protons (positive charges).

magnetic resonance imaging (MRI): computerized images of internal body tissues made by the effect of radio waves on the body's atoms in a magnetic field.

membrane: a material that separates a cell from its surroundings and controls which materials can enter and leave a cell.

mitochondria: the powerhouse of the cell. It helps obtain energy from food and then stores the energy.

mutation: a sudden change in one of the inheritable characteristics in a living being.

nucleus: the part of a cell that contains DNA and directs overall cell activities.

ophthalmology: the science of the eye's structures, functions, and diseases.

pacemaker: invented by Wilson Greatbatch in 1958, it is an electrical device that is surgically implanted into a living being to assist the beating of the heart.

pharmacopoeia: an official book that lists and describes medicines, herbs, and other substances.

radioactive: a state of giving off radiant energy in the form of particles or rays.

radioisotopes: radioactive isotopes.

ribosomes: structures in a cell needed to manufacture proteins from amino acids.

stethoscope: a medical instrument used to listen to sounds produced in the body. A stethoscope helps people make a diagnosis.

transfusion: the transfer of blood from one living thing into the body of another.

vaccination: weakened or dead germs administered to a body to cause it to develop cells that protect the body against catching a particular disease.

X-ray: a picture made with electromagnetic radiation of a part or parts of a living being.

More Books to Read

Bill Nye the Science Guy's Big Blast of Science. Bill Nye (Perseus Press)

The Body. Young Scientist Concepts and Projects (series). Steve Parker (Gareth Stevens)

Discoveries That Changed Science. Lois Markham (Raintree/Steck Vaughn)

The Disease Book. Margaret O. Hyde (Walker)

DNA Pioneer: James Watson and the Double Helix. Joyce Baldwin (Walker)

The Health Revolution: Surgery and Medicine in the Twenty-First Century (Beyond 2000). David J. Darling (Dillon)

The History of Health and Medicine. Jenny Bryan (Raintree/Steck Vaughn)

The Human Body (series). Andrew Llamas (Gareth Stevens)

The Living World. Record Breakers (series). David Lambert (Gareth Stevens)

Our Bodies. Under the Microscope (series). John Woodward and Casey Horton (Gareth Stevens)

Those Mean Nasty Dirty Downright Disgusting But...Invisible Germs. Judith Rice (Redleaf Press)

Videos to Watch

Diagnostic Radiology. (Fairview Audio-Visuals)
A Drop of Blood. (Bart Media Group)
The Gene. (Hawkhill Associates)
Genetics and Plant Improvement. (Encyclopædia Britannica Educational)
The Human Heart Machine. (PBS Video)

Human Pharmacy. (Discovery Channel)
Patterns of Inheritance. (MTI Film and Video)
Radiation. (Hawkhill Associates)
Vaccines and Preventive Medicine. (Films for the Humanities and Sciences)
The Very Special You. (Marsh Media)

Web Sites to Visit

kidshealth.org/kid/

www.innerbody.com/htm/body.html

www.bonus.com
 (Choose *Explore* and *What's Inside?*)

cnn.org/health

www.kidsvista.com/Sciences/
 biology.html

www.healthfinder.gov

Some web sites stay current longer than others. For further web sites, use your search engines to locate the following topics: *cloning, Marie Curie, DNA, genetics, health,* and *vaccines.*

Index